AKHENATEN'S EGYPT

SHIRE EGYPTOLOGY

Cover illustration
Akhenaten and his family worship the Aten, in a modern painting on papyrus.
(Courtesy of Bolton Museums and Art Gallery, Bolton Metropolitan
Borough Council.)

British Library Cataloguing in Publication Data.
Thomas, Angela P.
Akhenaten's Egypt. — (Shire Egyptology),
1. Egypt. Akhenaten, Pharaoh of Egypt
fl. 1379-1362 B.C.
I. Title
932'014'0924
ISBN 0-85263-973-2

Published by
SHIRE PUBLICATIONS LTD
Cromwell House, Church Street, Princes Risborough,
Buckinghamshire HP27 9AA, UK.

Series Editor: Barbara Adams

ISBN 0 85263 973 2.

First published 1988; reprinted 1996.

Printed in Great Britain by
CIT Printing Services, Press Buildings,
Merlins Bridge, Haverfordwest, Dyfed SA61 1XF.

Contents

Acknowledgements

I gratefully record my thanks to Mrs Julia Samson and to the late Professor H. W. Fairman, both of whom excavated at Amarna and whose knowledge and generosity have always been a source of great encouragement.

I wish to thank those who have helped in the preparation of this book and particularly with the illustrations. The Petrie Museum of Egyptian Archaeology, University College London, have allowed me to reproduce photographs from their archive and I am grateful to the Curator, Barbara Adams, for providing me with the illustrations and for other help and support. Photographs of material from the tomb of Tutankhamun appear by kind permission of the Griffith Institute, Ashmolean Museum, Oxford. Photographs of officials' tombs and work at Amarna are reproduced by courtesy of the Committee of the Egypt Exploration Society. Photographs of items in the Bolton Museum collection appear by permission of Bolton Museums and Art Gallery and Bolton Metropolitan Borough Council. Acknowledgement is also made to W. J. Murnane and Penguin Books for the chronology.

4

List of illustrations

Chronology

After W. J. Murnane, *The Penguin Guide to Ancient Egypt*, 1983.

Predynastic	before 3150 BC	
Early Dynastic	3150 - 2686 BC	Dynasties I to II
Old Kingdom	2686 - 2181 BC	Dynasties III to VI
First Intermediate Period	2181 - 2040 BC	Dynasties VII to XI
Middle Kingdom	2040 - 1782 BC	Dynasties XI to XII
Second Intermediate Period	1782 - 1570 BC	Dynasties XIII to XVII
New Kingdom	1570 - 1070 BC	Dynasties XVIII to XX

1570 - 1293	*Dynasty XVIII*
1570 - 1546	*Ahmose*
1551 - 1524	*Amenophis I*
1524 - 1518	*Tuthmosis I*
1518 - 1504	*Tuthmosis II*
1504 - 1450	*Tuthmosis III*
1498 - 1483	*Hatshepsut (?)*
1453 - 1419	*Amenophis II*
1419 - 1386	*Tuthmosis IV*
1386 - 1349	*Amenophis III*
1350 - 1334	*Amenophis IV/Akhenaten*
1336 - 1334	*Smenkhkare*
1334 - 1325	*Tutankhamun*
1325 - 1321	*Ay*
1321 - 1293	*Horemheb*
1293 - 1185	*Dynasty XIX*
1293 - 1291	*Ramesses I*
1291 - 1278	*Seti I*
1279 - 1212	*Ramesses II*
1185 - 1070	*Dynasty XX*
1182 - 1151	*Ramesses III*

Third Intermediate Period	1070 - 664 BC	Dynasties XXI to XXV
Late Period	664 - 332 BC	Dynasties XXVI to XXXI
Graeco-Roman Period	332 BC to AD 395	Ptolemies and Roman Emperors

Akhenaten's Egypt

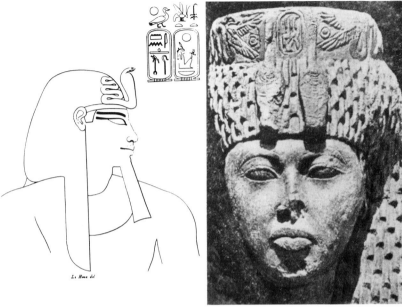

1. (Left) Head of Amenophis III at the temple of Luxor. (From Champollion, *Monuments de l'Egypte et de la Nubie*, volume IV, 1845, plate CCCXXXVI.)
2. (Right) Head of Queen Tiye in green steatite, found at the temple of Hathor at Serabit el-Khadim, Sinai. (From Weigall, *The Life and Times of Akhnaton*, 1922, facing page 72.)

3. Amenophis III as the victorious king in his chariot on a limestone stela from West Thebes. (From Petrie, *Six Temples at Thebes*, 1897, plate X, courtesy of the Petrie Museum.)

1
Introduction

Akhenaten was the second son of Amenophis III, a ruler of the Eighteenth Dynasty of kings in Egypt. At his birth he was named Amenophis after his father and he kept this name as he grew to manhood. Little is known about his childhood and youth, but his development and personality were a product of his experiences during his father's reign. Amenophis III (figure 1) was crowned king of Egypt in c.1386 BC. His family, who were from Thebes in the south, had ruled over the Egyptians for nearly two hundred years, during which the country had steadily become more prosperous and her reputation abroad had grown. As a child, Amenophis III had no doubt learnt about the exploits of those of his illustrious predecessors who had succeeded in securing an empire for Egypt which comprised Nubia in the south and an overlordship of Palestine and Syria in the east. The plunder of war, the tribute from foreign local rulers to their Egyptian overlord and increased trade had brought considerable wealth to the gods and their temples, the king and his family, courtiers and officials. Other nations in the Near East — the Babylonians, Hittites and Mitannians — had recognised Egypt's important position as a world power and had established diplomatic relations with her.

Amenophis III had entered into a great inheritance, when he was probably scarcely in his teens. An Egyptian king would be provided with a royal household of officials and wives, but he required a chief royal wife, a consort who would share his great role and present him with a son and heir and a daughter to be royal heiress. It had become a common practice in the Eighteenth Dynasty, whenever possible, for the son and heir to marry his sister and transmit the succession through both the male and female lines. Amenophis III, however, had no sisters. Although he implies that he chose his chief wife, it is likely that a suitable young lady was selected for him. Her name was Tiye (figure 2) and she was the daughter of an official named Yuya, a master of horses, and his wife, Thuya.

The accession of the king and the choice of Tiye as chief queen were marked by the issue of a large commemorative scarab. Four more large scarabs were issued in the early years of the reign recording the king's activities: hunting wild animals, his diplomatic marriage to Gilukhepa, a Mitannian princess, and the creation

4. Amenophis III, on the right, presenting offerings to the god Amun, on the left, from a limestone stela, West Thebes. (From Petrie, *Six Temples at Thebes*, 1897, plate X, courtesy of the Petrie Museum.)

5. Amenophis III offering to an image of himself on a relief scene at the temple of Soleb in Nubia. (From Lepsius, *Denkmaeler aus Aegypten und Aethiopien*, Abteilung III, 1849-59, 87b.)

of a lake for Queen Tiye. There was a campaign to Nubia in year 5 led by the king's viceroy (figure 3), and a small expedition may have been sent to Syria. The situation in Asia, however, gave little obvious cause for concern and Amenophis III contented himself by handling this through correspondence, exchanges of gifts, threats and setting one local ruler against another to maintain his overall supremacy. He concentrated on projects within Egypt, constructing a royal residence — a series of palaces at Malkata in Thebes — and adding to and building temples throughout Egypt and Nubia. Most of his reign of 38 years was peaceful and the empire seemed firmly held together.

Amenophis III was concerned with the status of the king, who in his imperial role ought to be an absolute ruler in control of civil, religious and military affairs. He may have considered that the temples and estates of the god Amun at Thebes had received enough of the riches of empire to pose a threat to the king in certain circumstances (figure 4). To counter this he appointed to high posts officials who came from the Delta or Memphis in the north, men who were loyal to their king and less likely to manipulate the income of any temple for political gain. He also began to promote the interests of a god who until his reign does not seem to have had a special priesthood or temples. That god was the Aten, the physical disk of the sun, which since the Middle Kingdom had been a symbol of divinity linked with the king. During the Eighteenth Dynasty Aten had emerged as a god who could be depicted as hawk-headed or as a winged sun disk with arms outstretched. The development of Aten as an aspect of the sun-god Re is significant for Re was the prominent deity of earlier times when kings had enjoyed absolute power. Since then many deities had been attached to Re, including Amun as Amun-Re.

Amenophis III, therefore, sought to identify the Aten as a particular cult of the king, a process which had been under way in the reigns of his father and grandfather, but which now became more positive with temples and a priesthood created for the god. To emphasise his own divinity further, Amenophis III was deified and statues of him were worshipped in various temples. At the temple of Soleb in Nubia a relief scene depicts him worshipping an image of himself (figure 5). Normally deification began when the king died and joined the gods. These measures were not directed against the cult of Amun or any other god but were part of a wider political struggle being waged by the crown. To the ordinary Egyptian at the time little of this would have been apparent or, indeed, important. Amenophis III's extensive

6. The Colossi of Memnon, statues of Amenophis III, which flanked the entrance to his mortuary temple at West Thebes. (From Lepsius, *Denkmaeler*, Abteilung I, 91.)

building programme, the wealth of the empire, the religious festivals and his jubilees in years 30, 34 and 37 might have been remote for many of his people but they were still clear enough evidence of his greatness. The private thoughts of those in the higher echelons of power are unknown.

Towards the end of his reign Amenophis III became more aware of his earthly mortality. In year 36 a statue of the goddess Ishtar of Nineveh was sent to him by King Tushratta of Mitanni, apparently for the second time. If this was a statue with healing powers, Amenophis III was probably in poor health. His mortuary temple and tomb at West Thebes were nearing completion, if not already finished (figure 6). During the 38th year of his reign the king died. He was about fifty years old. His burial was undoubtedly one of the richest interments to be made in the Valley of the Kings, but very little has survived.

Amenophis III, who had presided over the zenith and elegance of the empire and whose name would long be remembered, was mourned throughout Egypt and in particular by his family. He had a large number of wives, including several foreign princesses, and many children. However, the important members of his

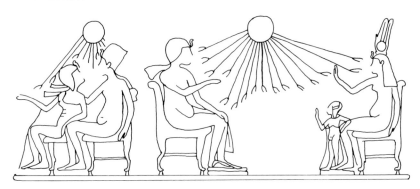

7. Amenophis IV and Nefertiti on the left and Amenophis III and Tiye on the right with their daughter, Beketaten, in a scene on the lintel in the tomb of Huya at Amarna. (After Davies, *Rock Tombs of El Amarna III*, 1905, plate XVIII.)

family were his chief queen, Tiye, and her offspring. Tiye had given birth to at least seven children, including two sons and five daughters. The eldest son, Tuthmosis, named after his grandfather, died during his father's reign. It was perhaps intended that he should marry the eldest daughter and royal heiress, Sitamun. Sitamun received the title of king's great wife from Amenophis III but whether she actually became her father's wife is unclear. Her position was possibly that of a dowager princess. The succession devolved upon Tiye's second son, Amenophis, who had not expected to be king and who is better known by the name Akhenaten, which he would choose for himself.

8. Head of Amenophis IV in the temple of Luxor. (From Weigall, *The Life and Times of Akhnaton*, 1922, facing page 80.)

2
Amenophis IV at Thebes

Amenophis IV became king in the shadow of a famous father and was faced with the dual task of controlling the empire and ruling his own land effectively. He was a young man, but old enough to possess estates, and was already married and a parent. Although the orthodox view is that he succeeded to the throne on his father's death, it is often argued that he was joint ruler or co-regent with his father for at least eight to nine years, or, more probably, eleven to twelve years. If this was so and he began the dating of his kingship on becoming co-regent, it must affect any assessment of his seventeen-year reign and implies that his sole rule was relatively short. The institution of co-regency was not unusual in Egypt and at certain periods was fairly common. In general, co-regencies were not intended to be of long duration but served to ensure the smooth transfer of power from a king to his chosen successor. Double datings occur for Middle Kingdom co-regencies and reveal that the junior king dated his reign from the time that he became co-regent. Double dates, however, are not given in the New Kingdom.

The evidence for a co-regency of Amenophis IV and his father rests partly on a number of objects inscribed with both their names, some of which date to the second half of the son's reign, and partly on the depiction of both kings in scenes in the tombs of officials at Amarna and Thebes and on reliefs at the temple of Soleb (figure 7). In all cases the names and representations of Amenophis III could be memorial and do not necessarily imply that he was living. He would be worshipped as a dead king, especially by his son and by his widow, Queen Tiye, who was still alive in the twelfth year of her son's reign. In addition there is documentary evidence. A number of papyri from the site of Kahun record the simple business transactions of a cowherd named Mesy and are dated from year 27 of Amenophis III to year 4 of Amenophis IV, a period of approximately fifteen years if there was no co-regency. Certain documents are signed by the same witnesses and it is debated whether, given life expectancy at the time, the documents could cover such a period, though this is certainly not impossible.

Even more debate surrounds a letter, sent to Egypt by Tushratta, king of Mitanni, on hearing of the death of Amenophis III, to express his sympathy and to establish relations with the new king. The letter, written on a clay tablet in cuneiform, the diplomatic language at that time, would not have reached its destination very quickly. On receipt, the back of the letter was endorsed with a note in hieratic stating that Amenophis IV was in Thebes when it arrived and giving the date. This date has given rise to speculation as the tablet is broken at that point. What remains of the date is the number two indicating year 2 of the reign, but there is enough room before the two to restore a ten, thus making the date year 12. This is difficult evidence and has to be weighed against another, undated, letter, to Amenophis IV from Suppiluliumas, king of the Hittites, in which he refers to when Amenophis III was alive and, in welcoming the son to power, says, 'Now you, my brother, have ascended the throne of your father', clearly implying that the father is dead. At Amarna, where building work started after year 4 of Amenophis IV's reign, two pottery sherds from wine jars were found inscribed with dates of the years 28 and 30. These years are from Amenophis III's reign and, if there was no co-regency, the wine jars were twelve to fourteen years old when brought to the site. It is unlikely that wine in porous jars would remain drinkable for this long, although the vessels may have been emptied and reused a number of times before they were broken.

Taken as a whole, the evidence for a co-regency between Amenophis IV and his father is inconclusive. If Amenophis III decided to associate his son with him on the throne, there seems little reason for him to have done so twelve or even eight years before his death. He was still at the height of his powers and celebrated the first jubilee of his reign in year 30. By the 35th or 36th year, when his physical health perhaps began to fail, he may have become anxious to secure the succession and taken his son as co-regent for about the last two years of his reign.

The early events of Amenophis IV's reign indicate that there was either no co-regency or one which was fairly brief. In year 1 of his kingship he ordered that work should continue on the decoration of two pylon gateways constructed by his father at the temple of Amun-Re at Karnak, Thebes (figure 8). The new king was obviously living at Thebes and it would have been appropriate for him to complete any of his father's unfinished projects. The relief scenes which were carved on one of the pylons depicted Amenophis IV in a traditional way, but with the Aten as a falcon-headed god (figure 9). Amenophis IV was adopting the policy of his father towards the Aten as the cult of the king. However, he may not have fully understood that a delicate

9. Aten as a falcon-headed god with Amenophis IV on a relief from Karnak. (After Aldred, *Akhenaten, Pharaoh of Egypt*, 1968, plate 45.)
10. Head of a colossal statue of Amenophis IV from East Karnak. (From Baikie, *A History of Egypt*, volume II, 1929, plate XIV.)

Akhenaten's Egypt

11. Amenophis IV in the short archaic cloak with the rays of Aten reaching down to him, and accompanied by priests during the jubilee ceremonies at Karnak. (After Aldred, *Akhenaten, Pharaoh of Egypt*, 1968, plate 49.)

balance needed to be maintained and that it required a man of considerable strength, perception and tolerance to carry out this policy successfully. Whether he possessed these qualities remained to be seen.

In his second year he gave instructions for four temples to be built for Aten at Thebes, in Karnak, outside the enclosure wall on the east of the Great Temple of Amun-Re. They were all more or less completed by the end of the fourth or beginning of the fifth year. These buildings were taken down at the end of the Eighteenth Dynasty and in the Nineteenth Dynasty. Their decorated blocks were used by Horemheb as filling for new pylon gateways at Amun's temple at Karnak, and by Ramesses II for the entrance pylon at the temple of Amun at Luxor and elsewhere. By the late nineteenth and early twentieth centuries erosion and damage had revealed some of these filling blocks in the Karnak and Luxor pylons. During restoration work at Karnak the pylons were dismantled, the filling removed and replaced with a modern core and the ancient outer walls rebuilt. By the mid 1960s about 45,000 blocks from the temples of Amenophis IV had been retrieved. The enormous task of photographing, studying and attempting to piece together the scenes from the blocks started in the 1970s in the Akhenaten Temple Project. Excavations were also undertaken at East Karnak, where colossal fallen statues of Amenophis IV had been found in the 1920s (figure 10). More blocks and the foundations of one of the temples were discovered, proving that this was its original site.

This temple was named the Gempaaten (meeting the Aten) and had a large rectangular court open to the sky, surrounded by a roofed colonnade and adorned with colossal statues of Amenophis IV.

The decorated scenes which had been in the temple showed a jubilee celebrated by the king in his second year and perhaps this marked his accession to sole rule after a short co-regency (figure 11). A jubilee or *sed* festival normally took place after thirty years of rule and such an early celebration is unusual. The ceremony, which probably lasted several days, was an ancient ritual in which the king demonstrated that he was still physically and mentally fit to rule and then received the allegiance of the whole land. For his part the king ran a course symbolically encircling his country, to prove his physical power, although by this period the runner was a chosen athlete rather than the king himself. The ritual was enacted before officials from all the districts and the gods of Egypt, whose statues had been brought from near and far to be placed in shrines. The king in his role as high priest of every cult presented offerings to the gods and was accepted by each one as worthy to rule. He was then re-crowned and the officials brought their offerings and affirmations of loyalty to him.

The scenes of the jubilee of Amenophis IV in year 2 follow the traditional ritual but differ from it in one very important respect. The shrines for the gods which are depicted all contain images of the king beneath the disk of Aten. Priests in procession carry the standards of the gods, but the famous deities do not seem to be present. Aten as the sun disk appears at the top of relief scenes and therefore the figure of the king below is more noticeable and the centre of attention. In traditional scenes figures of the king and god were equals standing together or the king might kneel to the deity. Here, by a paradox, the god has been elevated but has become inanimate and thereby the king achieves prominence. This appears entirely deliberate.

Of the other three temples to the Aten at Karnak, one called the *Hwt-Bnbn* (House of the Benben) was built for the king's chief queen, Nefertiti. The Benben stone in the shape of a pyramid was sacred to the god Re at Heliopolis, but in this temple it was shown as an obelisk, perhaps because Tuthmosis IV, the grandfather of Amenophis IV, had erected an obelisk to Re-Harakhty in the Amun temple at Karnak. In the scenes of the temple, Nefertiti is shown making offerings to the Aten, a role which normally belongs to the king, which indicates her high position in religious terms during these years at Thebes (figure

12). She was accorded the title Nefer-neferu-Aten, 'beauty of the beauties of Aten'. Nefertiti was fortunate in that she was beautiful and also very graceful. The king, by contrast, was not handsome according to the standards of the time, a fact which he emphasised almost perversely in his statues and reliefs in the early years (figure 13). Even allowing for a certain amount of exaggeration, his face was somewhat long and thin and had a degree of gauntness about it. His lower jaw stuck out but not in a strong way. His figure was hardly heroic, as his shoulders and chest were narrow, his abdomen, hips and thighs wide and his lower legs slim. Perhaps acutely aware of his physical appear-

12. Nefertiti and her daughter, Merit-aten, offer to Aten on an interior gateway of the *Hwt-Bnbn* at Karnak. (After Redford, *Akhenaten, the Heretic King*, 1984, figure 6.)

13. The gaunt and exaggerated features of Amenophis IV from one of his colossal statues at Karnak. (From Baikie, *A History of Egypt*, volume II, 1929, plate I.)

ance, he determined not to be represented in an idealised way and went to the other extreme, occasionally seeming almost grotesque. At least, no doubt intentionally, this had the effect of setting him apart from most mortals.

From the earliest Aten temple reliefs at Karnak it is clear that the king and queen already had a child, a daughter called Meritaten, who was born at the beginning of the reign, if not before. Two more daughters, Meketaten and Ankhsenpaaten, were born by the end of the fourth year. All are described quite unequivocally as king's daughters of his body, born of the great royal wife, Nefertiti. The king had other wives in his harem but they are not named in the reliefs. The years at Thebes had been fully occupied with the jubilee, the building of Aten temples there and at Heliopolis, Memphis and in Nubia, at sites which were already connected with deities. Aten had no special cult centre of his own. It was time to make new plans.

14. Boundary stela of Akhetaten showing the king, queen and two of their daughters offering to Aten at the top and with the text dedicating the site below. (From Breasted, *A History of Egypt*, 1909, figure 140.)

15. Plan of the central part of Akhetaten showing the Great Temple to Aten on the right and on the left the king's house, the small temple to Aten and the king's official palace. (From Lepsius, *Denkmaeler*, Abteilung 1, 64.)

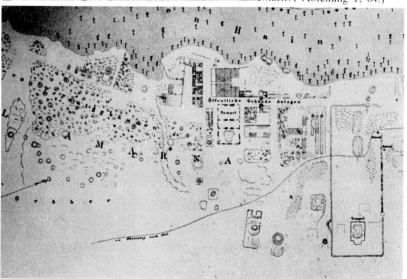

3
Akhenaten at Amarna

Years 4-12

In the fourth year of his reign the king decided to find a virgin site for the cult of Aten and discovered a suitable place in Middle Egypt, more or less equidistant between Thebes and Memphis. That site, commonly known today (after one of its villages, El Till, and the Beni Amran people of the district) as Tell el-Amarna, was named Akhetaten, the horizon of Aten. Here the king intended to build a great city for Aten and his decision was commemorated by the erection of three stelae marking the boundaries of the proposed city. Their inscriptions are damaged by long exposure but a broken part near the end refers to evil things heard and possibly to evil priests. Some officials may have been critical of royal activities, but the king controlled the army and it is perhaps significant that military attendants are much in evidence in the Aten temple reliefs at Thebes and that the area of Akhetaten was an enclosed and defensive site.

Work began immediately on the new city. In the fifth to sixth year of the reign the central part of the city was more or less completed and it was at this time that the king changed his birth name from Amenophis to Akhenaten, in honour of the god. In year 6 a further eleven stelae were set up at Akhetaten marking the final boundaries (figure 14) and the oath of dedication on them was renewed in year 8 when the king again inspected the boundaries and an inscription recording this was added to them. By then the city was expanding rapidly (figure 15) and perhaps now the king finally transferred his seat of government to Akhetaten and made it his main residence. He had already ordered that his name in the form of Amenophis in the Aten temples at Thebes should be altered to Akhenaten and that further work on those temples should cease. Unlike his predecessors Akhenaten extended his policy to an attack against the cult of Amun and to a certain extent against the cults of other gods. Their names were erased in temples and their worship suppressed. How widespread this suppression was is difficult to judge but it would have struck mainly at the officials and priesthoods of the gods concerned. Such a step gave the king immense political power. In more practical terms there were also economic advantages. If temples were closed and their priesthoods disbanded, the estates and income of those cults could be repossess-

16. Relief scene of rows of offerings of cattle, bread, fruit and flowers for the Aten temple, from Amarna. (Petrie excavation photograph, courtesy of the Petrie Museum.)

ed by the crown. Akhenaten needed more revenue in order to build his city and provide lavish offerings for the new temples to Aten (figures 16 and 17). The property which he acquired by these means was administered by his own officials and not, as before, by local ones. Government, therefore, became more centralised and the officials and priests, all educated men, who were adversely affected by the changes, could not do other than accept them. For the ordinary Egyptians the religious implications lay not so much in the closing of temples, which were the province of god, king and priests, but in the ceasing of the festivals and processions of the gods, in which they had participated and which were an important feature of social life. If Aten was to remain a remote god, just for the king, and did not celebrate regular festivals throughout the land, the general population might become dissatisfied.

Thoughts on such matters were perhaps far from the king's mind as he gazed on his new city in year 8 and considered the future. Before long the names of the Aten were changed in order to purify them and include references only to Re, the sun-god. This occurred between years 8 and 12 and is often ascribed to year 9. The earlier epithet of Aten in year 2, 'he who is in jubilee', became 'Lord of Jubilee', which might imply that Akhenaten celebrated a second jubilee then.

Perhaps by year 9, and certainly by year 12, his official family had grown. Nefertiti had given birth to three more children, all girls, named Neferneferuaten, Neferneferure and Setepenre. The king and queen now had six daughters (figure 18). Amongst the wives in Akhenaten's harem was a Mitannian princess, Tadukhi-pa, who had arrived in Egypt as a diplomatic alliance for

17. Nefertiti presenting offerings to Aten on a relief from Amarna. (Petrie excavation photograph, courtesy of the Petrie Museum, UC. 401.)

18. The princesses Neferneferuaten and Neferneferure on a wall painting from the king's house in the central city, Amarna. (Petrie excavation photograph, courtesy of the Petrie Museum.)

19. Head of Kiya on a relief from Hermopolis. (After Cooney, *Amarna Reliefs from Hermopolis*, 1965, plate 18b.)

20. Akhenaten and Nefertiti with their six daughters at the reception of foreign tribute in year 12, on a scene in the tomb of Meryre II at Amarna. (After Davies, *Rock Tombs of El Amarna II*, 1905, plate XXXVIII.)

21. The presentation of tribute from the east in the tomb of Meryre II at Amarna. (After Davies, *Rock Tombs of El Amarna II*, 1905, plate XXXIX.)

Akhenaten's father not long before the latter's death. Little is known about the other wives, which is not unusual, except for a lady named Kiya (figure 19). She has become known only since 1959, from a small number of objects and reliefs which bear her name, representations of her and inscriptions which appear to be connected with her. She has no particular title but is described consistently as the greatly or much beloved wife of the king. Her name is associated with both the early and late forms of the name of Aten and she was therefore a favoured wife over a number of years. The logical explanation for her position, which is borne out by other instances relating to secondary wives in the Eighteenth Dynasty, is that she was a principal wife who had a child or children by Akhenaten, and more importantly that she was the mother of a son. Nefertiti and her children, as the official family, were shown in relief scenes, whereas a secondary wife and her children would have remained in the background. While Nefertiti continued to bear children, there was always the possibility that she might have a son, and, if so, that child would have taken precedence as heir over an elder son by another wife.

The official family are all shown together for the last time in the twelfth year, when Akhenaten held a great ceremony for the reception of tribute from abroad (figure 20). Scenes of this dated event, in all probability a high point of the reign, appear in the tombs at Amarna of the officials Huya and Meryre II. Representatives from north, south, east, west and the islands of the Mediterranean presented their gifts to the king. Akhenaten was accompanied by Nefertiti and his daughters, four of them being depicted in the tomb of Huya and all six in that of Meryre II. It is not clear whether this ceremony is connected with the celebration of the king's second or third jubilee. The scenes record only the foreign tribute, which would have been dedicated to Aten and may have been combined with a jubilee.

Foreign affairs

Akhenaten has often been accused of dreaming at Amarna, taking little interest in foreign matters and therefore being responsible for the loss of Egyptian prestige and territory in the empire. The scenes of foreign tribute in year 12 may be exaggerated and inevitably are flattering from the Egyptian point of view (figure 21), but they do indicate that the standing of the Egyptian king and Egypt had survived and that the overlordship of Palestine and Syria was still held. The archives of foreign correspondence at Amarna reveal the considerable diplomatic activity of the period, although the letters give a somewhat one-sided picture as Akhenaten's replies are not preserved.

In the south in Wawat and Kush (Nubia) the king's policy was firm: to protect trade and the routes towards the important gold-mines in the eastern desert. Any difficulties with local rulers or tribes were dealt with by force. These campaigns, which were on a relatively small scale, were often conducted by the king's viceroy, the king's son of Kush, although the victory, glory and plunder were claimed by the king. One such campaign led by the viceroy took place under Akhenaten in Akuyta near the gold-mines and was recorded on a stela by the viceroy at Buhen.

In the north the situation in Palestine and Syria was far more complex, particularly in northern Syria. The intelligence service ensured that information was constantly transmitted to the king and the relevant officials, but the distances were great and circumstances changed quickly. Problems arose with and amongst the local rulers, especially in north Syria. Like his father, Akhenaten probably employed mainly diplomatic means in dealing with complaints and appeals, only occasionally resorting to threats and military activity. Egypt was, however, not the only great power with an interest in Syria. To the east lay the kingdom of Mitanni, once the enemy of Egypt in the days of Tuthmosis I and Tuthmosis III, although the two nations had since come to a general understanding about their respective spheres of influence in Syria and had sealed the friendship with diplomatic presents, including the gift of Mitannian princesses to Tuthmosis IV and Amenophis III. This alliance created a loosely united bloc at the eastern end of the Mediterranean, leaving the Hittites or Hatti to the north and Assyria and Babylon to the south-east

Akhenaten does not appear to have fostered relations with Tushratta, king of Mitanni. The Hittite king, Suppiluliumas, who had begun to rule during the time of Amenophis III, communicated with Akhenaten and sent gifts, establishing an alliance. Suppiluliumas was an able and determined ruler intent on territorial expansion. He attacked the Mitanni, defeating Tushratta, who was assassinated not long afterwards, and swept into northern Syria, taking areas previously under Mitannian influence. The Mitanni were reduced to a barrier state between the Hittites and the slowly increasing might of Assyria and eventually were completely overcome by the Hittites. The rulers in northern Syria were divided, some accepting Hittite over-lordship, whilst others sought to encourage conflict between the great powers for their own gain.

22. Akhenaten taking his mother, Queen Tiye, and the young Beketaten on a visit to the temple of Aten. From the tomb of Huya at Amarna. (After Davies, *Rock Tombs of El Amarna III*, 1905, plate IX.)

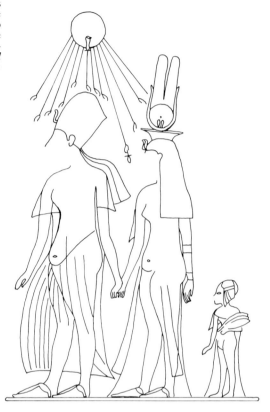

The position was difficult as, astutely, the Hittites had not attacked areas of Egyptian influence. North Syria was far away and the fate of its rulers may have seemed unimportant. Akhenaten and his advisers no doubt considered the affair carefully, but effective military aid would have required sending, at great cost, an army of ten to twenty thousand men and becoming embroiled in an unwelcome war with the Hittites. By the time the army arrived, north Syria might already be conquered. It would have been politic to despatch a large force to coastal and south Syria as a demonstration of strength, but this was not done and the reputation of Akhenaten and of Egypt was diminished as a result. Encouraged by Akhenaten's apparent inactivity, there were a number of smaller incidents of unrest in Palestine and Syria, but these were dealt with reasonably effectively. Akhenaten was unfortunate to preside over this

hegemony of empire during a troubled period. He could have
been more positive in his foreign policy in the north, but the
empire was not yet lost, as the reception of foreign tribute in year
12 shows.

Years 12-17

In about year 12, perhaps to view the foreign ceremony,
Akhenaten's mother, Queen Tiye, visited Amarna. With her was
her youngest daughter, Beketaten, born near the end of her
husband's reign and still a girl. Tiye's visit is recorded in scenes in
the tomb of Huya, who was the superintendent of her household
and estates. Tiye was entertained by her son and daughter-in-law
and was taken by her son to see the shrine, the shade of Re, at the
temple of Aten which was dedicated to her (figure 22). Whether
these scenes suggest that Tiye had come to live at Amarna is hard
to determine. Her household there had been established and
staffed, but her main links were with Thebes and she may have
spent her time at a number of residences.

So far no real disaster had occurred, but between years 12 and
15 Akhenaten appears to have suffered several personal blows. It
may be significant that a plague starting in Mitanni had travelled
to coastal Syria and that foreign envoys had recently visited the
Egyptian court, for not long afterwards Meketaten, the second
daughter of Akhenaten, died. The royal tomb at Amarna was
hastily prepared for the burial of the princess and some subsidiary
rooms were decorated. In a poignant scene Akhenaten and
Nefertiti lean united in their grief over the body of their child
(figure 23). Fragments of the granite sarcophagus of Meketaten
were discovered in the Amarna royal tomb in modern times. The
three youngest daughters of Akhenaten and Nefertiti, Neferneferuaten, Neferneferure and Setepenre, do not appear again
and it is possible that both they and Queen Tiye also died around
this time.

The sequence of events and indeed the events themselves
which followed are not clear. Various interpretations are feasible,
and from these it is necessary to present a broad summary of
different versions as an account of the end of Akhenaten's reign.

In the first version Nefertiti is often thought to have died by
year 14, although there is no clear evidence to support this. The
existence of part of a shabti or funerary figure bearing her name
from Amarna and a small amount of jewellery, including a gold
inscribed ring found near the royal tomb in 1882, do not indicate
that she died before her husband. The fragments of sarcophagi

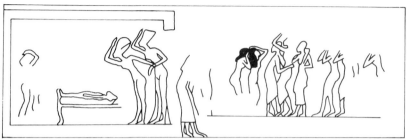

23. Akhenaten and Nefertiti mourning the death of their daughter, Meketaten, in the Royal Tomb at Amarna. (After Aldred, *Akhenaten, Pharaoh of Egypt*, 1968, plate 87.)

24. Head of Kiya from a purification scene. (After Cooney, *Amarna Reliefs from Hermopolis*, 1965, plate 17.)

found in the tomb were not hers and she does not seem to have been buried there.

It was perhaps in the later part of the reign at buildings associated with her that Kiya (figure 24) was sometimes depicted with Akhenaten and seems to have had by then two young daughters named Meritatentasherit and Ankhsenpaatentasherit after the king's two eldest surviving daughters. Their choice of names may appear strange but it is suggested that this was in honour of the two official princesses who would be married to Kiya's sons. By about year 14 Kiya had either died or retired from view because the king's eldest daughter, Meritaten, was old enough to take on the role of a queen. That Kiya was dead is likely as inscriptions of her name were erased at the north palace and Maru Aten and recarved for Meritaten. On relief blocks from Amarna, reused and found at Hermopolis, Kiya's name was replaced by that of Meritaten and in some cases by that of

25. The figures of Akhenaten
and his co-regent on the stela of
Pase from Amarna. (After
Aldred, *Akhenaten, Pharaoh of
Egypt*, 1968, plate 81.)

Ankhsenpaaten. In about year 14 or 15, in order to secure the
succession, Meritaten, the royal heiress, became the wife of a
young man named Smenkhkare, who was designated as heir and
co-regent. If Akhenaten had a son or sons, he would surely have
raised one as successor. Smenkhkare and Meritaten were possibly
the same age, born at the beginning of the reign or a year or two
before. Perhaps here was Kiya's first child, the reason why she
had been much beloved by the king. Proof is lacking but the
co-regency itself is generally accepted and rests on representations of two kings together, often unnamed, and on inscriptions
where both are named. On one stela two kings seated beneath the
disk and rays of Aten are shown in an affectionate pose, which
accords with Akhenaten's love for his family and might imply a
relationship like father and son (figure 25). The co-regent's
coronation name was Ankhkheperure, but his birth name or
nomen apparently occurs in two forms as Smenkhkare (mainly at
Amarna and on a relief from Memphis) and as Neferneferuaten
(at Amarna, on certain objects, and at Thebes). It would seem
that the young man was called Smenkhkare, but that as sole king
he took the name Neferneferuaten and that he journeyed to
Thebes.

During the final years of Akhenaten's reign economic and administrative problems may have arisen and caused dissatisfaction. These problems might well have been attributed to the disturbance in the divine order and been seen as a sign of the displeasure of the great gods who had been neglected. Smenkhkare was no doubt advised by those more experienced and aware of the situation to make certain religious and political gestures. This was done or at least started. The highest year date known for the co-regent Neferneferuaten is year 3 in a graffito for a priest Pawah written in the Theban tomb of another priest, Pere. Pawah was a scribe of Amun in the house of Ankhkheperure/ Neferneferuaten at Thebes.

The highest date known for Akhenaten is year 17, during which year he died and was laid to rest in the Royal Tomb at Amarna. The parts of his burial equipment found in the tomb include fragments of his granite sarcophagus, alabaster canopic chest, shabtis, boxes and chests (figure 26). His co-regent became king, but perhaps survived him for less than a full year, and then died at the age of about nineteen to twenty and was possibly buried at Thebes. His young wife, Meritaten, apparently had no children and whether she survived him is not known.

26. Head of a shabti figure of Akhenaten in syenite from the Royal Tomb at Amarna. (Courtesy of the Petrie Museum, UC. 007.)

In the second version of events at the end of Akhenaten's reign his co-regent Smenkhkare has another identity, a view which has emerged since 1973. The co-regent does not claim to be the king's son but does claim to be beloved of him. In the few instances where the two rulers are shown together it is on very affectionate terms and at one time they were thought to represent Akhenaten and Nefertiti although the fact that both wore king's crowns seemed to contradict this. However, Nefertiti is shown in reliefs wearing certain crowns and headdresses which kings did wear (figure 27). Early in the reign her name was lengthened to Neferneferuaten-Nefertiti and her name was duplicated at Amarna in two cartouches in the same way that the name of the king was written in double cartouches. The coronation name of the co-regent, Ankhkheperure, is in certain cases found written with a *t*, which indicates the feminine, and with the epithet 'beloved of Akhenaten', and the name Neferneferuaten taken by the co-regent was one originally accorded to Nefertiti. Therefore it was argued that Akhenaten's co-regent was not a young man and prince but his queen, Nefertiti, who was raised to the kingship as Ankhkheperure Neferneferuaten and who later, as sole ruler, took the name Ankhkheperure Smenkhkare. On the basis of the names the evidence for Nefertiti as co-regent may be favourable but it is not conclusive. It could be suggested that the co-regent might have taken on the religious role formerly held by Nefertiti and therefore have assumed her title and epithets. The only dated instance of the co-regent's name on its own is in the form Neferneferuaten in year 3 at Thebes, as though this was the later name; and there is no identified example of Nefertiti clearly wearing the blue khepresh crown, which the co-regent did wear and which was a definite crown of kingship.

What the two versions of events above do not account for is the interesting fact that the name Ankhkheperure Smenkhkare is not linked in any instance to the name Neferneferuaten with its epithets of Akhenaten or the feminine form of Ankhkheperure. It would be most unusual for a queen to be co-regent with her husband while he lived, because a co-regency was the means of transferring power, preferably to a son, without any problems. A queen might be appointed as regent on her husband's death to act on the behalf of a successor who was very young. The evidence would suggest that Smenkhkare and Neferneferuaten, while sharing the same prenomen, were not one person but two individuals. Smenkhkare, a young prince and probably the son of Akhenaten, was married to Meritaten and appointed co-regent

27. Nefertiti wearing her distinctive tall crown with ram's horns, disk and plumes on a relief from Amarna. (Petrie excavation photograph, courtesy of the Petrie Museum.)

but died before or in the same year as Akhenaten. The next successor was another young prince, Tutankhaten, who was married to Akhenaten's third daughter, Ankhsenpaaten. He was only eight or nine years old and therefore Nefertiti became regent for him, a role which as Neferneferuaten she fulfilled for about three years, undertaking negotiations at Thebes to repair the divine order, until either she died or Tutankhaten reached an acceptable age to rule alone.

28. Relief head of Akhenaten from Amarna. (Petrie excavation photograph, courtesy of the Petrie Museum.)

29. The official Ay is congratulated after receiving rewards from the king, which include gold collars and a pair of gloves. From Ay's tomb at Amarna. (After Davies, *Rock Tombs of El Amarna VI*, 1908, plate XXX.)

4
The royal family

Relationships within the royal family at this period appear to have been very complicated. Apart from immediate family, the king's following might include cousins, relatives of wives, children of officials, distant relatives and so on. Through marriage a whole series of interlocking relationships was formed and many of the king's officials were probably related to the royal family in some way or other. This is not particularly surprising but is difficult to prove because such relationships were rarely stated. Any view of the royal family tends to be subjective and there are a number of interpretations of the known facts, the gaps in the evidence and possible events.

The clear basic information is that Akhenaten (figure 28) was the son of king Amenophis III and his chief queen, Tiye, daughter of Yuya and Thuya; that he married as his chief queen Nefertiti, who had a sister, Mutnodjmet; that he had another wife, Kiya; and that Nefertiti had six daughters.

The family of queen Tiye may have had more than one connection with the royal family and therefore an influential position. Tiye's father, Yuya, was from Akhmim, where he held priestly posts in the service of the god Min. It is thought that he was perhaps the brother of Mutemwiya, mother of Amenophis III. He held the titles of god's father and overseer of the king's horses. The title of god's father, rather than denoting a priestly office, may mean in this context 'father-in-law of the king'. Yuya and his wife, Thuya, were given the honour of burial in a tomb in the Valley of the Kings, where their bodies still rested when the tomb was discovered in 1905. They had a son, Anen, who was a priest of Amun and Re Atum. This brother of queen Tiye was buried in a tomb at Qurna, Thebes. He did not refer to his royal links, even though he was the brother-in-law of Amenophis III. However, Thuya names him as her son on her wooden sarcophagus and probably he died before her.

It is conceivable that Yuya and Thuya had another son. The official Ay in the reign of Akhenaten held the titles of god's father, overseer of the king's horses, fan-bearer on the right hand of the king and scribe of the king (figure 29). The first two titles were the same as Yuya's and, as sons often inherited their fathers' offices, perhaps Ay was the son of Yuya. Ay was to dedicate a chapel to the god Min at Akhmim, implying that he or his family came from there, and Yuya was from Akhmim. However, the fact that Ay was god's father could mean that he was the father-in-law of Akhenaten. Ay is often regarded as the likely father of Nefertiti and her sister, Mutnodjmet. Nefertiti never calls herself king's daughter or sister, does not appear to be in the direct royal line and never names her parents, and nor does Mutnodjmet. Ay's wife was a lady named Tey, who had been the nurse of Nefertiti. She was not, therefore, Nefertiti's mother, but whether she had brought the girl up as Ay's second wife after the mother's death or had served as nurse in an important family in which Nefertiti was a daughter is difficult to say. The tomb which was prepared for Ay at Amarna, although unfinished, was large and well decorated and Mutnodjmet is depicted in it. In the scene where Ay received honours from Akhenaten and Nefertiti, it is unusual to find that his wife, Tey, standing behind him, was honoured as well. Nevertheless, this could be simply a mark of the queen's affection for her nurse when the latter's husband was rewarded, rather than an occasion concerning the queen's father and stepmother. Ay's career, however, was to continue after the reign of Akhenaten and rise to greater heights.

The pedigree of Akhenaten's wife Kiya is unknown, but she seems likely to have come from an official family which had links with the royal household. Because of the discovery of a number of inscriptions relating to her, the view was put forward that it was Kiya who became co-regent with Akhenaten, on account of his love for her. Though Kiya may be described as greatly beloved by the king, this should not be taken at face value as a romantic statement, but rather seen as an acknowledgement of her position as a secondary wife and in particular as the mother of royal children.

The origin of Akhenaten's young successors, Smenkhkare and Tutankhaten, has been discussed over many years. They are often considered to be princes and probably brothers. It is possible to argue that they were the sons of Amenophis III by Tiye or his eldest daughter, Sitamun, but only by accepting a long co-regency between Amenophis III and Akhenaten. Without a co-regency of nine to twelve years this explanation is physically impossible and the evidence for a co-regency is not conclusive. The only other king who could be their father is Akhenaten, an easier solution, but Nefertiti seems to have had no sons. It is not unreasonable to suppose that they were Akhenaten's sons by another wife and the most obvious candidate is Kiya. Before he became king the young Tutankhaten called himself 'king's son of

30. The entrance to Tomb 55 on the right in the Valley of the Kings in 1907. (From Weigall, *The Glory of the Pharaohs*, 1923, facing page 136.)

his body', something which Smenkhkare does not appear to claim, but neither of them stated the names of their parents.

The co-regency of Akhenaten and Smenkhkare and the difficulties surrounding it have already been discussed. The body of Smenkhkare may have survived, although the identification is not certain. In 1907 Theodore Davis, an American who was excavating in the Valley of the Kings at Thebes, found the small Tomb 55 (figure 30). It is a rock-cut tomb with steps leading underground, a sloping passage and one room with a niche in one of its walls. The contents appeared to be in some disorder, and stones and water falling into the room in the past had caused some damage. On the floor lay a wooden inlaid and gilded coffin of a royal woman but with the uraeus of kingship later added to the brow. The coffin, with parts of its inscriptions erased, had rested on a low wooden bed but this had collapsed, cracking the coffin lid and forcing it partly away from the base to reveal a poorly preserved wrapped body. The niche contained a set of alabaster canopic jars. The panels of a large gilded shrine lay against one wall or on the floor and one panel was across the passage, as though abandoned on its way in or out. Other finds included four magical bricks of Akhenaten, a wooden casket, fragments of items of Amenophis II, Amenophis III and Tiye and clay sealings of Tutankhamun. The gilded shrine had been made for Queen Tiye by Akhenaten, but his figure had been mostly erased from it. Davis concluded that he had found the tomb and mummy of Tiye. However, the body in the coffin turned out to be that of a young man, with certain epiphyses not united and no abnormal characteristics, who had died at the age of nineteen or twenty (figure 31). Later comparisons with the body of Tutankhamun, whose tomb was found in 1922, revealed a physical resemblance between the two young men (figure 32), which

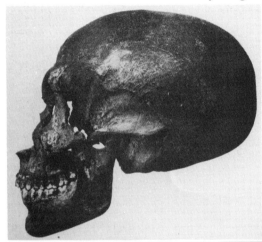

31. The skull of the young man in Tomb 55, thought to be Smenkhkare. (From Weigall, *The Life and Times of Akhnaton*, 1922, facing page 248.)

32. (Below) Head of Tutankhamun. (From Carter, *The Tomb of Tutankhamen*, volume 2, 1927, plate XXXI, courtesy of the Griffith Institute, Oxford.)

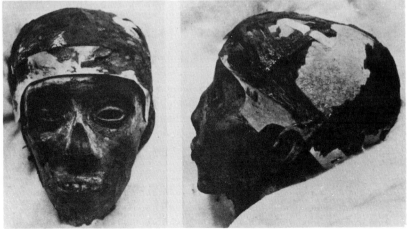

33. (Left) The head of Kiya on a canopic jar lid from Tomb 55, later altered for a king. (From Weigall, *The Life and Times of Akhnaton*, 1922, facing page 80.)
34. (Right) The gold vulture collar found on the head of the young man in Tomb 55. (From Weigall, *The Life and Times of Akhnaton*, 1922, facing page 248.)

might indicate that they were brothers, and therefore the body in Tomb 55 was identified as that of Smenkhkare. Various attempts to identify the body as that of Akhenaten have foundered because of the early age of death, and because disorders which delay aging of the bones involve sterility and Akhenaten had six daughters by Nefertiti alone.

The exact circumstances surrounding the burial may never be clear, but those who placed the young man in his coffin knew his identity. The coffin was that of a royal lady and was originally made for Kiya but was altered at some trouble to receive the body of a king. The canopic jars were also originally made for Kiya (figure 33). These items might represent an appropriate choice if Smenkhkare was Kiya's son. On the body itself was a broad collar of gold and electrum with inlays of coloured glass. On the head was a gold vulture collar bent round to serve as a diadem (figure 34). The clay sealings of Tutankhamun in the tomb are evidence that the body was placed here during his reign as he would have

been responsible for the burial, but his predecessor had had little
time to prepare a tomb and all the equipment. Some of
Smenkhkare's intended burial equipment, including a gilt shrine,
canopic jar lids and coffinettes and plaques from mummy bands,
as well as objects of Akhenaten probably made in his early years
at Thebes, were to be used some years later for the burial of
Tutankhamun (figure 35), as though all had been kept in storage.
The magical bricks of Akhenaten in Tomb 55 were perhaps
suitable protection for his co-regent, whose sole reign had been
non-existent or very short. The shrine of Tiye and other
fragments might have been gathered as family mementoes for the
burial. The tomb had been entered later, items removed and
inscriptions on the coffin and shrine partly erased. Whether, as
suggested, the tomb originally had other occupants who were
taken out, like Akhenaten brought from Amarna or, more likely,
Tiye, is not very clear. The only person found in the tomb was left
with his identity destroyed.

   The successor of Akhenaten and Smenkhkare, the child
Tutankhaten, kept his birth name for three to four years while he
had a regent. In his third year he left the city of Akhetaten and
moved to Memphis. Very soon a restoration stela was erected at
the temple of Amun at Karnak in Thebes stating that the gods
and their shrines were neglected and in ruins and therefore the
land was in confusion. Here was the confession and the king
promised to make images of the gods, to restore their temples
and shrines and to provide income, property and staff to serve
them. He changed his name to Tutankhamun and that of his wife
to Ankhsenamun. Before long the city of Akhetaten was deserted
by royalty and officials. These decisions were probably not made
by the young king but by those who had recognised the need to
make them.

   Tutankhamun ruled into his tenth year and died at the age of
about eighteen. The discovery of his virtually intact tomb in the
Valley of the Kings by Lord Carnarvon and Howard Carter in
1922 is well known. The tomb's magnificent and largely traditional equipment included a number of items connected with his
childhood and family (figure 37) but did not reveal his parentage.
It is interesting to note that when Howard Carter removed the
final wrappings and first saw the face of Tutankhamun (figure 38), he was immediately struck by the likeness to
portraits of Akhenaten and thought that Smenkhkare and
Tutankhamun might be the sons of Akhenaten by a lesser wife.

   Tutankhamun left no heir. A later Hittite account records that

35. (Left) One of the gold canopic coffins, which held the mummified internal organs, from the tomb of Tutankhamun, but originally made for Smenkhkare. (From Carter, *The Tomb of Tutankhamen*, volume 3, 1933, plate LIV, courtesy of the Griffith Institute, Oxford.)
36. (Right) Head of a granite statue of Tutankhamun from Thebes. (From Baikie, *A History of Egypt*, volume II, 1929, plate XXIII.)

a widowed Egyptian queen, probably Ankhsenamun, wrote to Suppiluliumas asking for one of his sons in marriage, an amazing request. The Hittite king was suspicious but the story seemed true and so he sent a son called Zannanza, who was assassinated on his journey. Relations between the Egyptians and Hittites deteriorated as a result of the incident. This episode is a strange one, on which Egyptian sources are silent. Whatever intrigues took place, it was the official Ay, who had served Akhenaten and was the vizier of Tutankhamun, who became king. Aside from his possible connection with the royal family, there are other recorded instances where the vizier, as highest state official, took the throne in the absence of an heir. Ankhsenamun was seen no more. Ay's queen, shown in scenes in the tomb he now prepared in the Valley of the Kings, was Tey, the former nurse of Nefertiti and his wife since the days at Amarna. Ay was not young and his reign was short, about four years, and he probably had no living son. The throne passed to Horemheb, king's deputy and commander of the army, who had risen to high office in the reign of Tutankhamun. His queen was a lady named Mutnodjmet, but whether she was the sister of Nefertiti is uncertain. Horemheb concerned himself with the administration and the army, usurped some of the monuments of his predecessors, which was not an unusual occurrence, and may have reigned for over twenty years.

37. The gold-covered and inlaid throne of Tutankhamun. The scene on the back shows the king and his wife beneath the rays of Aten. (From Carter and Mace, *The Tomb of Tutankhamen*, volume 1, 1923, plate LXIII, courtesy of the Griffith Institute, Oxford.)

38. The gold funerary mask of Tutankhamun, a portrait which reveals the resemblance in facial features between various members of the royal family of the period. (From Carter, *The Tomb of Tutankhamen*, volume 2, 1927, frontispiece, courtesy of the Griffith Institute, Oxford.)

It was after Horemheb that the reaction against Akhenaten and the rulers associated with him was unleashed. In the king-list in the temple of Seti I at Abydos, which named the kings of Egypt from the First Dynasty down to the reign of Seti, Amenophis III was followed by Horemheb; Akhenaten, Smenkhkare, Tutankhamun and Ay were struck from the official records. Inevitably Akhenaten suffered the worst treatment. His temples were dismantled and much of their stone reused, his city was partly destroyed and he was referred to as 'the enemy'. The cult of the Aten survived into the Ramesside period, but the deity's most loyal promoter had been consigned to oblivion.

39. (Left) The early name of Aten written in double cartouches being offered by Nefertiti to the god. (Petrie excavation photograph, courtesy of the Petrie Museum.)

40. (Below) Part of a limestone back pillar from a statue of Akhenaten with the late name of Aten. From the house of Panehesy at Amarna. (Courtesy of Bolton Museum, Bol. 30.24.17.)

5
Religion and art

Religion

During the reign of Amenophis III the position of Aten as a form of the sun-god Re had been somewhat ill-defined. Akhenaten sought to remedy this and early in his reign Aten was named 'Long live Re-Harakhty, he who rejoices in the horizon is his name, as the sunlight which is Aten'. Aten was shown as a falcon-headed god in the earliest reliefs of Akhenaten at Karnak, but the king quickly determined a standard iconography for Aten as a sun disk with uraeus and with rays extending from the disk ending in human hands holding the sign of life. Aten was given a titulary like the king and the god's name was written in double cartouches (figure 39). By this process the god became king of gods and the king the god, both sharing similar qualities and being described with the same epithets. Between years 8 and 12 the names of Aten were altered to exclude any reference to gods other than Re and Aten and were written as 'Long live Re, ruler of the two horizons, he who rejoices in the horizon is his name as Re the father who returns as Aten' (figure 40). The concept of the god thus became exclusive, containing Re, the father; Aten, the physical expression of the father, visible to man; and the king, son of Re and Aten, 'the unique one of Re' and 'the good child of the living Aten', their manifestation on earth. Akhenaten was the living Aten as the god had no cult image and he worshipped Aten and Re, but lesser mortals worshipped him as the divine mediator between men and god (figure 41).

The concept of Aten appears to lack the female element so often seen in the families of deities in Egypt comprising a god, goddess and their godly child. However, Aten and Akhenaten are called father and mother of all, the king refers to himself as father and mother of his people and in some of his early statues is hermaphrodite. The queen became the obvious female element and she plays an important role in the worship of Aten. The raising of Aten as a state god was quite acceptable and his development, temples and form of worship with offerings followed conventional practices. The king's plan differed from the norm in his steady elimination of all deities except Re, Aten and himself, denying the existence of other gods by not mentioning them and, in some cases, by deliberately acting against them. These hardly seem to be the actions of a

41. (Left) Meryre, high priest of Aten, raising his arms in adoration to king and god in his tomb at Amarna. (After Davies, *Rock Tombs of El Amarna I*, 1903, plate XXXVII.)
42. (Right) Nefertiti pours wine into the king's cup, from a scene in the tomb of Meryre II at Amarna. (After Davies, *Rock Tombs of El Amarna II*, 1905, plate XXXII.)

monotheist, visionary or messiah born out of his time, but more those of a political opportunist, dogmatically and rationally imposing his will. A king who was high priest, sole mediator and synonymous with one god would hold truly absolute power, but the god would need to fulfil all religious requirements and it was in this respect that Aten and Akhenaten were to fail.

The Egyptian pantheon of gods was complex, encompassing the many aspects of divine nature and providing the order in society. Life on earth and life after death were subject to moral standards to preserve that order. The religion of Aten contained no ethical teaching. The hymn to the Aten, the text of which appears in officials' tombs at Amarna, is a poem extolling the sun, based on earlier sun hymns. Comparisons between the hymn and the later Psalm 104 of the Hebrews are often made and each represents the expression of independently developed and similar ideas. The hymn does not offer rules for a good life or any notion of a judgement at death. Previously the life after death had promised the worthy Egyptian an eternal existence with the gods in the sky, sun, stars, earth and underworld. Aten offered an afterlife which seemed negative by comparison, in which, during the day, the sun drew the deceased's *Ba* or soul from his body to stay near the altar at his temple, but at night there was nothing: for the living and the dead merely slept in the cold darkness. Atenism might be logical and beneficial to the king, but it was too remote and did not provide what his educated and non-educated subjects wanted and expected: on the contrary, it seemed to offend against the established order. The king might state that he lived by truth, but it was not the same as the truth which had sustained the divine and the human in Egypt for centuries. The king's policy created social problems. Those problems were resolved after Akhenaten's death by restoring the gods to their proper roles, thus reinstating the accepted order and then tackling the other difficulties. Aten retained his position as the divine sun disk and it was Akhenaten who was judged solely responsible and punished.

Art

The distinctive style of the reign arose as a means of depicting Aten and the worship of Aten by the royal family. Some of the features, including the flowing lines of figures and drapery, the softening of the face, the effeminacy exhibited by males and the more relaxed and informal poses, were not sudden innovations but had been developing gradually. The king and his officials are no longer lean and ambitious for conquest but well dressed and fed and enjoying the luxuries of empire. These trends and the traditional forms were translated into what is, above all, a personal art of the king (figure 42). The representations were not for general consumption, as the interiors of temples were the province of royalty and priests, the tombs were the places of the dead, and the royal buildings were the quarters of the royal family and entourage.

The iconography of Aten as a sun disk made necessary certain changes in the composition of scenes. When a king was depicted with a deity in human or anthropomorphic form, the figures could be balanced against each other. Akhenaten was balanced by the figure of the queen, the princesses, an offering table, another figure of himself or by bowing priests or servants in various combinations. In tomb scenes relating to the rewarding of officials or other occasions, like visits to the temple or the reception of foreign tribute, the importance of the large figures of the king and queen is emphasised and yet also balanced by those of the officials, servants and activities depicted on a much smaller

43. Women and servants of the temple honour the visit of the king and queen in the tomb of Meryre at Amarna. (Photograph by Davies, courtesy of the Egypt Exploration Society.)

scale to complete the composition (figure 43). In general the decoration was carried out quickly and inevitably most attention and care was concentrated on the royal figures. Relief scenes tended to be executed in incised relief in which the outlines of the figures and inscriptions were cut into the stone and details carved within the outline. This took less time than raised relief, which involves taking down the background to leave figures and inscriptions standing out from it. In order to focus attention on the upper part of the king's figure and on Aten above, the traditional proportions used for the human figure were revised. This was an innovation. The part of the body above the navel was lengthened and this makes the legs seem foreshortened. In the more extreme style of the early years the width of the abdomen and hips is most noticeable, but later the proportions of head and hips became more realistic and therefore more attractive. The fingers were also lengthened, imparting great delicacy to any gesture of the hands. The method of representing the king applied to the queen, the royal family and in a broad sense to officials and servants. Sculpture in the round was carved in accordance with the revised proportions and to the modern eye is perhaps easier to appreciate than the profile view offered in relief scenes (figures 44 and 45).

The worship of Aten affected the content of scenes in officials' tombs, as many funerary scenes were no longer appropriate and the repertoire sanctioned by the king was somewhat limited. Royal scenes are much in evidence, including offering to Aten, visits to the temple, the palace, the reception of foreign tribute, the official honoured or invested by the king and congratulated by his servants and friends, prayers to the Aten and the hymn to Aten. The king and his activities dominate the decoration. Officials, servants and attendants are shown bowing low from the waist, but with faces raised to their king and god (figure 46). This is a characteristic pose which looks uncomfortable but which is also held by attendants running along, unless this is artistic convention. The great official in his tomb lifts his arms in

45. (Right) Statuette of Nefertiti or a princess in quartzite, from Amarna. (Courtesy of the Petrie Museum, UC. 002.)

44. (Below) The studio of the chief sculptor, Auta, from a scene in the tomb of Huya at Amarna. (After Davies, *Rock Tombs of El Amarna III*, 1905, plate XVIII.)

46. (Above) The bowing pose of officials, priests and attendants in royal scenes, from the tomb of Mahu at Amarna. (Davies, *Rock Tombs of El Amarna IV*, 1906, plate XII, A, courtesy of the Egypt Exploration Society.)

47. (Left) Tenre, the wife of Meryre, in his tomb at Amarna. (Davies, *Rock Tombs of El Amarna I*, 1903, plate IV, courtesy of the Egypt Exploration Society.)

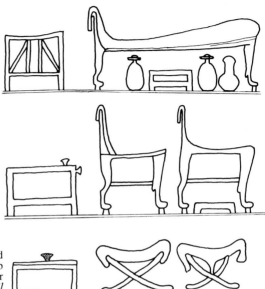

48. Funerary furniture and equipment in a scene in the tomb of Huya at Amarna. (After Davies, *Rock Tombs of El Amarna III*, 1905, plate XXIV.)

adoration to Aten and the king. In some tombs the official's wife is depicted (figure 47), but except for names and titles little is revealed about the life and family of the official. By comparison officials' tombs of the Eighteenth Dynasty before Akhenaten contained scenes of their families, careers, leisure pursuits, banquets with friends, estates, servants and funeral ceremonies, with few references to the king. Most of the officials' tombs at Amarna were unfinished. The tomb of Huya, steward of Queen Tiye, contained funerary scenes which are simple and show the mummy, the priest, the mourners and the funeral procession carrying the furniture and offerings to the tomb (figure 48).

The decoration which Akhenaten planned for the royal tomb was perhaps not dissimilar to that in the officials' tombs and would have included scenes of the Aten, himself and his family, royal events and the burial ceremony. Although many reliefs in the officials' tombs have suffered damage, the royal tomb, which was not finished, was devastated to the extent that little survived of its scenes except for those concerned with the death of Meketaten.

The domestic art of the reign was based on the traditions of the Eighteenth Dynasty, but the themes were often treated in a freer naturalistic way. Parts of palaces had plastered walls, ceilings and floors painted with patterns or nature scenes of considerable charm. Such scenes were a feature of royal residences of the period and in a less detailed and adapted form appear in private houses of all kinds.

Akhenaten's legacy in artistic terms was that his revised proportions for royal figures continued to be used for a short time in royal tombs, although not in any other relief scenes or sculpture, and many of the stylistic features of the art of his reign persisted for much longer, well into the Ramesside period.

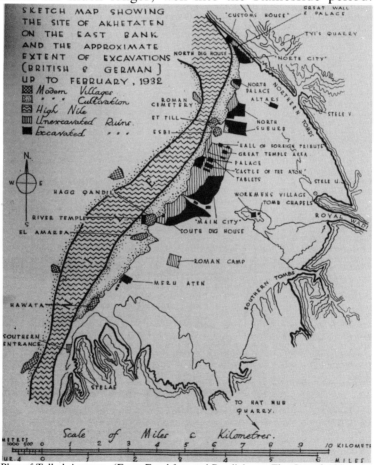

49. Plan of Tell el-Amarna. (From Frankfort and Pendlebury, *The City of Akhenaten II*, 1933, plate I, courtesy of the Egypt Exploration Society.)

6
The city of Akhetaten

The city which Akhenaten built for Aten and as a royal residence and capital at Tell el-Amarna was situated on the east bank of the Nile (figure 49). The area chosen was approximately 7 miles (11 km) long, forming a semicircular bay from the river, and was ringed by desert cliffs. There was little arable land on the east bank to sustain the city, which lay alongside it on the edge of the desert, but crops could be grown across the river on the west bank and supplies could be brought in from outside. The surveying, measuring and planning of the major roads and buildings presented few problems for there were no earlier structures on the site to take into account. Construction started with the heart of the city, the central official quarter, with its temples, palaces and administrative buildings. The Great Temple to Aten and a smaller Aten temple were constructed of stone and as sun temples they contained unroofed courts and processional ways leading to the altars, which were also open to the sky. The walls were decorated with relief scenes and the temples provided with statues.

Most of the secular buildings, as was normal, were built mainly of mud-brick with elements like column bases, lintels and door frames of stone, and columns, doors and roofing timbers of wood. By the side of the temples were their storehouses and stretching behind were the various government offices. Between the two temples was a house of the king, his state office, which was eventually connected by a bridge across the road to the vast official palace complex with its halls, courts, colonnades and gardens (figure 50). The facade on to the river and part of the palace is now under modern cultivation. Within the palace statues of the king and queen in granite and quartzite, relief scenes, wall paintings, decorative glazed faience inlays, elegant furniture and colourful hangings, matting and cushions created an impression of magnificence which can only be imagined from the surviving fragments (figures 51 and 52). This central quarter had been planned in a hurry and was just as hastily built. Alterations and additions were made within a very short time.

To the south of the central quarter was a residential area in the southern or main city which was probably the next part completed as it contained the houses of the great officials like the vizier, Nakht (figure 53), the army commander, Ramose, and the

50. Scene of the royal palace or a part of it in the tomb of Meryre at Amarna. (After Davies, *Rock Tombs of El Amarna I*, 1903, plate XVIII.)

priest, Panehesy. Their houses were like villas and square in plan with a vestibule, reception rooms, storerooms, large central hall or living room with a hearth, private apartments, bathroom, a courtyard with a well, and a garden. An upper storey around the higher central hall and reached by stairs probably provided further family rooms and in all a large house might have had about forty rooms. Kitchens and servants' quarters were sited in the grounds away from the main house as were the granaries, storehouses, offices, workshops and stables. The grounds were enclosed by a wall to ensure privacy and effectively made these houses like estates. These estates were also planned, although less important houses soon began to fill the spaces between and around them. The smaller, and even the poorest, houses in the city were also square in plan, built around a central living room, but the number and extent of the rooms varied according to the status of the owner. Richer properties had stone doorways and a number of rooms with columns; in other houses wood or painted plaster doorways and a few columns had to suffice. Nearly all houses were surrounded by a wall, which in some cases enclosed barely more than a yard outside the house with an area for

51. Design of a painted floor in the great official palace with themes taken from nature. (Petrie photograph, courtesy of the Petrie Museum.)

52. Fragments of glazed faience inlays and tiles from the great palace. (Courtesy of Bolton Museum.)

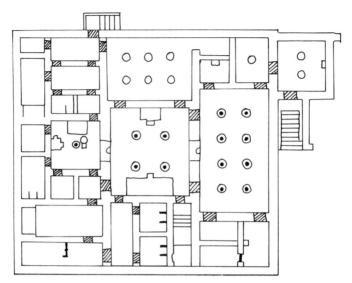

53. Plan of the large, square main house of the vizier Nakht, laid out around a central hall. (After Peet and Woolley, *The City of Akhenaten I*, 1923, plate III.)

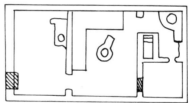

54. Plan of a rectangular house in the workmen's village with a front room, living room, and bedroom and kitchen at the back with stairs to the roof. (After Peet and Woolley, *The City of Akhenaten I*, 1923, plate XVI.)

cooking and to store grain, whereas some enclosures were big enough to have outbuildings for cooking, servants and animals.

The interior of the house was usually decorated with painted or whitewashed ceilings and walls, and floors might be plastered and painted or tiled and painted. The quality of decoration depended on the size of the house. In the great houses sanitation usually included *en suite* bathrooms, at least for the master and mistress. The bathroom had what might be described as a manual shower with a stone slab on the floor on which to stand and stone-faced low mud walls around it. The water was brought in jars and poured on to the person and drained out through the slab into a container. Nearby was the lavatory, in effect an earth closet which had a lavatory seat of wood, pottery or stone above a big bowl of sand. Homes which did not have these facilities relied on bowls and pots, which had to be emptied frequently, well away from the house. Fitted furniture might include a low platform in the living room on which to sit, platforms in bedrooms for the beds and supports for shelves in storerooms. Movable furniture and furnishings ranged from the elegant inlaid chests for clothes, bedding and belongings, finely carved chairs, stools, low tables, low beds, patterned cushions, mats and glazed faience, painted pottery, stone and metal vessels to the basic chest, plain table, simple cushions and mattresses and a few pots.

To the north of the central quarter was a residential suburb of large houses, joined, as expansion accelerated, by smaller and finally humble houses, crowded in wherever they would fit. The overall plan, if there was one, was soon lost in the need for quick building and previous rubbish dumps were levelled for this. At the far north end of the site in the north city was the private residential palace with its gardens and service buildings. To the south of the north city was the north palace, a ceremonial structure completely planned and enclosed by a wall. It was not that large but many of its rooms were decorated with bright wall paintings of birds, fish and figures with patterned borders and friezes. Ceilings were painted with vine leaves and grape clusters. Only the late form of the Aten name occurs here, implying that it was built in the latter part of Akhenaten's reign and the paintings seem hastily executed. Near the palace are the remains of its storehouses and other structures presumably connected with it.

At the extreme south end of the city was another ceremonial palace or cult complex called the Maru Aten, which contained kiosks or shrines, rooms, gardens and a pool. This was decorated with stelae, statuary and paintings. To the east of the southern main city and some distance away was a workmen's village for those whose task was to cut out and decorate the royal tomb and those of the officials in their northern and southern groups in the desert cliffs. The village was enclosed by a wall but it later expanded to an area outside this. The men who lived here with their families were state employees and they were provided with little houses built in terraced rows on narrow streets (figure 54). The plan of the houses was not square but rectangular and each dwelling had a front room off the street, a central or main living room with a hearth, often supported by one wooden column or pole, and at the back two small rooms (figure 55). One of these

55. The living room with its hearth and raised platforms in a house in the workmen's village, looking towards the front of the house. (Peet and Woolley, *The City of Akhenaten I*, 1923, plate XVIII, 3, courtesy of the Egypt Exploration Society.)

was a bedroom and the other was a kitchen with stairs going up to the roof, where there was an upper storey, which perhaps comprised one room used for sleeping. The houses were decorated, but simply furnished. In the front rooms work like grinding grain or weaving was undertaken and these activities and the tending of animals extended into the street outside. Animal husbandry was an important aspect of village life both within and without its walls, and pigs, for example, were bred and raised, presumably for the city. Market gardening was another cottage industry.

When the city was abandoned as a royal residence in the reign of Tutankhamun, the royal buildings and officials' houses were obviously cleared first. The furniture and other contents were packed and in some cases reusable building materials were removed and the houses sealed. In the royal palaces and workshops sculpture no longer required was left behind. In the officials' houses there remained images of the king and queen, small and more ephemeral items, broken objects and things somehow forgotten. From the government offices anything current or recent was taken away, but in the records office cuneiform tablets of correspondence from the reigns of Akhenaten and Amenophis III were considered as dead files and left there. Papyrus copies of them in hieratic were probably taken for reference, but the originals were no longer needed. The smaller houses and the workmen's village were not vacated so quickly and more domestic items, household equipment and rubbish survived as a reminder of the busy lives of the inhabitants who occupied the city so briefly and contributed in their own way to its history (figures 56 and 57). Some time later Akhenaten's temples and palaces were taken down to reuse the stone or otherwise

56. (Right) Blue-painted pottery jar lid with lotus-petal motif from house V.36.10 in the north suburb. (Courtesy of Bolton Museum, Bol. 28.29.7.)

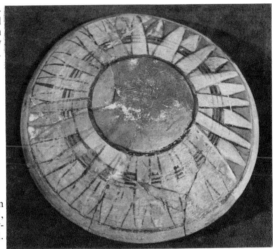

57. (Below) Basket lid from the workmen's village, House 3, main street. (Courtesy of Bolton Museum, Bol. 15.22.5.)

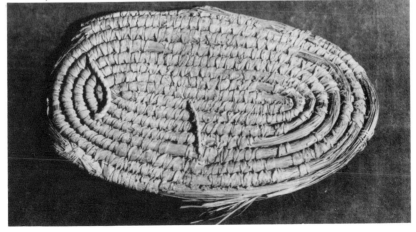

58. Limestone papyrus column fragment with part of the name of Akhenaten and the epithet 'great in his duration, king . . .' Probably from the great palace. (Courtesy of Bolton Museum, Bol. A.64.1967.)

despoiled and the bigger houses were plundered. The modest houses and the workmen's village escaped without much destruction. Gradually the roofs of the buildings fell in, their walls began to decay and they were filled with wind-blown sand.

The remains of the city and its rock tombs have attracted official and unofficial attention since the early nineteenth century. The royal tomb, the officials' tombs and the boundary stelae have been studied, copied and assessed. From the late nineteenth century until the 1930s parts of the city were excavated, but most areas were not completely cleared and some, for example the north palace and the north city, require far more detailed work. Since the 1930s the discovery of reliefs at Hermopolis, originally from Amarna, and the information gathered from the blocks and sites of the Aten temples at Thebes, have led to reinterpretations of aspects of Akhenaten's reign and the evidence from his city. In the late 1970s survey and excavation recommenced at Amarna with the advantages of modern archaeological technology and practice. In conjunction with the planning and survey, excavation was undertaken at the workmen's village, of which about half was cleared in the early 1920s, and new evidence unearthed about the houses, the areas in and around the village and the lives of the occupants. The work programme continues in the main city.

It is too early to say whether Amarna will yield substantial information for solving some of the problems surrounding Akhenaten's reign. It is an opportunity to learn more about the city, which can be said to be his major achievement, and to study the details of daily life in the late Eighteenth Dynasty. Like his predecessors, Akhenaten wished to live for eternity and for his name to be remembered (figure 58). In ancient times this was denied him, but many centuries later that wish has been fulfilled.

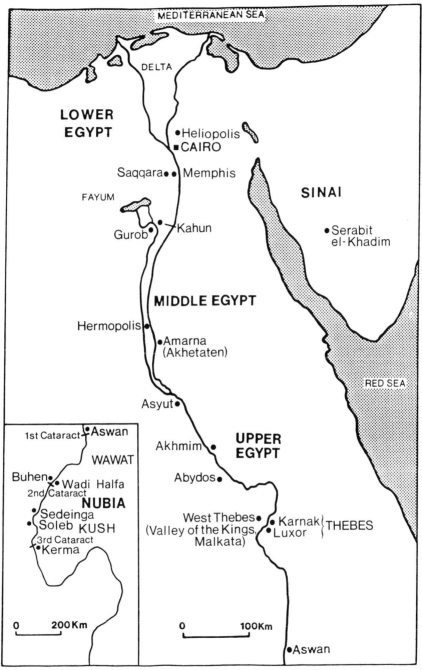

59. Map of Egypt, showing the location of sites mentioned in the text.

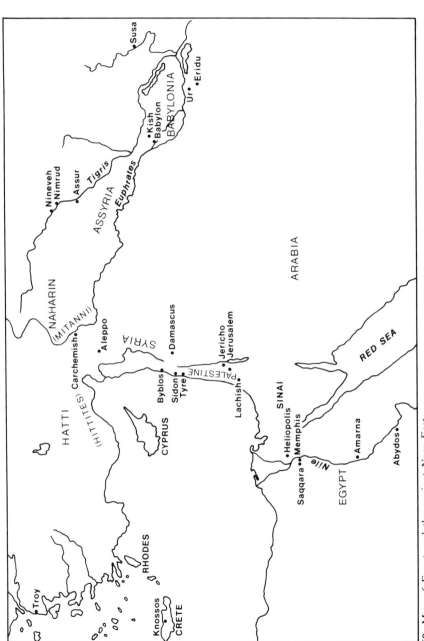

60. Map of Egypt and the ancient Near East.

7
Further reading

There is a great deal of published material, expressing many points of view, on the reign of Akhenaten, his family and successors. In addition to excavation reports and books, there are a large number of articles in journals. A detailed bibliography, by G. T. Martin, of books and articles in all languages can be found in *A Bibliography of the Amarna Period and its Aftermath* (Kegan Paul International, London, 1991). The list below refers to selected publications in English, excluding articles. The bibliographies in these works can be consulted for further references. The excavation reports include references to earlier work at the sites.

Excavation reports: Amarna

Davies, N. de G. *The Rock Tombs of El Amarna*, parts I to VI. Egypt Exploration Society, London, 1903-8. 1902-7 survey, photography and drawing of the scenes and inscriptions in the officials' tombs and on the boundary stelae.

Kemp, B. J., *et al. Amarna Reports* I to V. Egypt Exploration Society, London, 1984-9. The survey and excavation undertaken since 1977, still continuing.

Martin, G. T. 'The Royal Tomb at El-Amarna', in *The Rock Tombs of El Amarna*, part VII. Egypt Exloration Society, London; volume I, 1974; volume II, 1989. The tomb and its objects.

Peet, T. E.; Wooley, C. L.; Frankfort, H.; Pendlebury, J. D. S.; *et al. The City of Akhenaten*, parts I-III. Egypt Exploration Society, London, 1923, 1933, 1951. 1921-36 excavations including work in the workmen's village, Maru Aten, central city, north suburb, north palace and north city.

Petrie, W. M. F. *Tell el Amarna*. Methuen, London, 1894. 1891-2 excavation of the great palace, other official buildings and some houses.

Excavation reports: Hermopolis

Cooney, J. D. *Amarna Reliefs from Hermopolis in American Collections*. Brooklyn Museum, Brooklyn, 1965.

Roeder, G.; Hanke, R. *Amarna-Reliefs aus Hermopolis*, volumes 1 and 2. Hildesheim, 1969, 1978.

Akhenaten's Egypt

Excavation reports: Thebes

Carter, H. *The Tomb of Tutankhamen*, volumes I to III (volume I with A. C. Mace). Cassel, London, 1923, 1927, 1933. The discovery and clearance of Tomb 62, Valley of the Kings.

Davis, T. M.; Maspero, G.; *et al. The Tomb of Queen Tiyi.* London, 1910. 1907 excavation of Tomb 55, Valley of the Kings.

Redford, D. B. *The Akhenaten Temple Project*, volume II. Toronto, 1988.

Smith, R. W.; Redford, D. B. *The Akhenaten Temple Project*, volume I. Aris & Phillips, Warminster, 1977.

Selected books

Aldred, C. *Akhenaten and Nefertiti*. Brooklyn Museum, Brooklyn, 1973.

Aldred, C. *Akhenaten, King of Egypt*. Thames & Hudson, London, 1986.

Aldred, C. *Akhenaten, Pharaoh of Egypt*. Thames & Hudson, London, 1968.

Desroches-Noblecourt, C. *Tutankhamen: Life and Death of a Pharaoh.* London, 1963.

Giles, F. J. *Ikhnaton: Legend and History*. Hutchinson, London, 1970.

Kitchen, K. A. *Suppiluliuma and the Amarna Pharaohs*. Liverpool Monographs in Archaeology and Oriental Studies 5, Liverpool, 1962.

Mercer, S. A. B. *The Tell el-Amarna Tablets*, volumes I and II. Toronto, 1939.

Pendlebury, J. D. S. *Tell el-Amarna*, London, 1935.

Perepelkin, G. *The Secret of the Gold Coffin*. USSR Academy of Sciences, Nauka, Moscow, 1978. Discussion of Tomb 55 and Kiya.

Redford, D. B. *Akhenaten: The Heretic King*. Princeton University Press, Princeton, 1984.

Samson, J. *Amarna, City of Akhenaten and Nefertiti – Nefertiti as Pharaoh*. Aris & Phillips, Warminster, 1978. Evidence and discussion for Nefertiti as co-regent and king.

Weigall, A. *The Life and Times of Akhnaton*. Thornton Butterworth, London, 1922.

8
Museums

Many museums have material in their collections relating to Akhenaten and his reign. It is advisable to enquire about specific items and about the opening times of the museum before arranging a visit.

United Kingdom

Ashmolean Museum of Art and Archaeology, Beaumont Street, Oxford OX1 2PH. Telephone: 01865 278000.

Birmingham Museum and Art Gallery, Chamberlain Square, Birmingham B3 3DH. Telephone: 0121-235 2834.

Bolton Museum and Art Gallery, Le Mans Crescent, Bolton, Lancashire BL1 1SE. Telephone: 01204 522311, extension 2190.

Bristol City Museum and Art Gallery, Queens Road, Bristol, Avon BS8 1RL. Telephone: 0117 922 3571.

The British Museum, Great Russell Street, London WC1B 3DG. Telephone: 0171-636 1555.

Dundee Art Galleries and Museums, Albert Square, Dundee DD1 1DA. Telephone: 01382 432020.

Durham University Oriental Museum, Elvet Hill, Durham DH1 3TH. Telephone: 0191-374 2911.

Fitzwilliam Museum, Trumpington Street, Cambridge CB2 1RB. Telephone: 01223 332900.

Glasgow Art Gallery and Museum, Kelvingrove, Glasgow G3 8AG. Telephone: 0141-221 9600.

Hunterian Museum, The University of Glasgow, Glasgow G12 8QQ. Telephone: 0141-330 4221.

Liverpool Museum, William Brown Street, Liverpool L3 8EN. Telephone: 0151-207 0001.

The Manchester Museum, University of Manchester, Oxford Road, Manchester M13 9PL. Telephone: 0161-275 2634.

Petrie Museum of Egyptian Archaeology, University College London, Gower Street, London WC1E 6BT. Telephone: 0171-387 7050, extension 2884.

Royal Museum of Scotland, Chambers Street, Edinburgh EH1 1JF. Telephone: 0131-225 7534.

Swansea Museum, Victoria Road, Swansea, West Glamorgan SA1 1SN. Telephone: 01792 653763.

Australia
National Gallery of Victoria, 180 St Kilda Road, Melbourne, Victoria 3004.
Nicholson Museum, University of Sydney, Sydney, New South Wales 2006.
South Australian Museum, North Terrace, Adelaide, South Australia 5006.

Belgium
Musées Royaux d'Art et d'Histoire, Avenue J.F. Kennedy, 1040 Brussels.

Canada
Royal Ontario Museum, 100 Queen's Park, Toronto, Ontario M5C 2C6.

Denmark
Ny Carlsberg Glyptotek, Dantes Plads, 1550 Copenhagen V.

Egypt
Egyptian Museum, Tahrir Square, Cairo.
Luxor Museum, Luxor

France
Musée du Louvre, Palais du Louvre, 75003 Paris.

Germany
Ägyptisches Museum, Schlossstrasse 70, 1000 Berlin 19.
Ägyptisches Museum, Staatliche Museen, Bodestrasse 1-3, 102 Berlin.
Roemer-Pelizaeus Museum, Am Steine 1, 3200 Hildesheim, Niedersachsen.

Italy
Museo archeologico, Via Colonna 96, Florence.
Museo Egizio, Palazzo dell'Accademia delle Scienze, Via Accademia delle Scienze 6, Turin.
Museo Egizio, Vatican City, Rome.

Netherlands
Rijksmuseum van Oudheden, Rapenburg 28, 2311 EW Leiden.

Russia
A. S. Pushkin State Museum of Fine Arts, Ul Volkhonka 12, Moscow.
Hermitage Museum, St Petersburg.

Sweden
Medelhavsmuseet, Jarntorget 84, Stockholm.

United States of America
Brooklyn Museum, 188 Eastern Parkway, Brooklyn, New York, 11238.
Cleveland Museum of Art, 11150 East Boulevard, Cleveland, Ohio 44106.
Metropolitan Museum of Art, 5th Avenue at 82nd Street, New York, NY 10028.
Museum of Fine Arts, 465 Huntington Avenue, Boston, Massachusetts 02115.
University of Chicago Oriental Institute Museum, 1155 East 58th Street, Chicago, Illinois 60637.
University Museum, University of Pennsylvania, 33rd and Spruce Streets, Philadelphia, Pennsylvania 19104.
Walters Art Gallery, Charles and Centre Streets, Baltimore, Maryland 21201.

68

Index